# THE POSSESSIVE RELATIONSHIP

## Signals that you are in one and how to make a change

**THOMPSON JOHNSON**

# Table of contents

## CHAPTER FIVE

### CONCLUSION

# INTRODUCTION

A possessive relationship is one of rudeness and control, not a bit of jealousy. Here's how to sign and change: Ownership is not sweet. Not full of love and romance. That's not what makes a great love story. In fact, possessive relationships often lead to intense dysfunction, manipulation, and even abuse. There is nothing positive about possessive relationships, but many people seem to see them romantically. Thinking someone loves you seems adorable at first. But making someone happy is one thing, controlling, manipulating, or even endangering their desires is one thing. Ownership is not a fair or equal partnership. When one partner believes the other is theirs, intense fear of loss turns into anger and jealousy. Learning how to recognize this behavior is very important for your mental and physical health. Ownership is usually managed by one person. The reason for this may be a past betrayal. It may be low self-esteem. It could be anger issues or it could be due to a difficult childhood. A lot of things lead to this type of relationship. Being possessive in a relationship is not always the result of these circumstances. Many have cheated in the past and have had perfectly healthy relationships since. It is someone who is unable to overcome past trauma and whose actions are dominated by fear of pain and rejection. There is a lack of trust from the person who is possessive in the relationship. They don't trust their partners or others. As we said before, this is often due to a bad childhood or a lack of parental love. People who feel the need to control their partner have a desire to do so. Possessive relationships aren't just for people who fear losing their partner. They use this fear as an excuse to control their actions. This need for control takes precedence over any love that has ever existed.

Possessives use love as an excuse to control and stick to their partner. And the person on the other side does the same. Love is a wonderful thing. Exploiting it is dangerous. And it's used as an excuse for being the victim of a possessive relationship to explain to friends and family why they put up with their partner's controlling behavior, but it's probably not love.

Possessive relationships usually start out intense. It feels romantic and whirlwind. This is what makes the feeling of love so strong. But what seemed magical and amazing soon turns into control and manipulation. A possessive person uses this story as an example of love. They will say they want to control their partner because they don't want to lose them or because they feel they don't deserve them. They use their partner's appreciation for the good times to rectify the bad. And it works very often. They guilt their partners or manipulate them in myriad ways to maintain a possessive relationship under the guise of love. So is possessiveness a sign of love? No. It's a sign of weakness. This is a sign of low self-confidence and unreliability. The signs that you are in a possessive relationship range from obvious to subtle. Possessive people are often so good at disguising their actions as love and compassion that they don't see the signs. Manipulation is an integral part of ownership, so it's important to know that you're in an ownership relationship, even if it's sensible. If some or all of these behaviors sound familiar to you, it's time to do something about possessiveness in your relationship.

# CHAPTER ONE

## They get unreasonably jealous

One thing to get a little jealous when you see your partner excited about an attractive stranger...but usually, you trust your partner and let go. In a possessive relationship, that little bit of jealousy gets out of hand. Your partner will accuse you of being interested in someone just because you talked to them. They will be jealous of you working late because your work gets more attention than theirs. Basically, they get jealous of anyone or anything that distracts you.

## They Love-bombed

A love bomb is an attempt to win someone over with excessive gestures such as sending flowers, buying a gift, or being romantic out of nowhere. This may seem cute, but it is often done very quickly before the person even knows you. This is very often a precursor to abuse or manipulation. Starting a relationship with overwhelming affection can be flattering and arousing, but once involved, it can turn eerie and dangerous.

## They show up out of the blue

They may see this behavior as pampering or showing affection, but it's actually a way to check you out. One of my closest friends was in a long-distance relationship. Every time she told her boyfriend that we were dating, he called me to say hello. He just pretended to be kind and wanted to get to know her friend, but he did so to make sure she was where she really was. If she doesn't send it back immediately, he will. And he always insisted on talking to me on the phone if he really wanted to make sure I was with her, pretending he wanted to be friends with her.

## Feel guilty about being happy

If you call your partner after getting a promotion or having a great day, they'll let you down by accusing them of bragging about your struggles. Speak negatively about your job, claiming that you are robbing has nothing to do with them, so they struggle to be happy for you at the moment. They may even speak negatively about their friends and family.

# CHAPTER TWO

## Don't want to give space

All healthy relationships require some level of personal space and boundaries. But in a possessive relationship, that is hardly the case. When you need a relaxing day, they ask why you can't relax together. They want you to spend all your free time together and they will say that you are always hanging out with friends or that they haven't spent a night together all week.

## They need to know your schedule

When you go out without them, they want to know where you are, where you're going, and who you're with. You don't always have to know where you are. You can also request to share your location via your mobile phone. Trying to create boundaries and privacy can lead to accusations of lying to make you feel guilty for sharing such details.

## They don't promote growth or success

In a healthy relationship, partners motivate, inspire, and support each other to become better and more versatile people. They want each other to be better and happier. But in ownership, it's just the opposite. A possessive partner would rather limit you than deny you growth and encourage exploration.

## They text a lot

But when it becomes unnecessary and overkill,

there is a reason for it. They want constant communication with you. They need to know they have your attention. It's one thing to text about meal plans and memes during your lunch break, but if you need a quick response when they ask about your day, something is wrong.

# CHAPTER THREE

## They are all over social media

Possessive people post lots of pictures of you on social media. They want the world to know that you are theirs. Also, you can learn a lot about your online activities. If someone compliments your selfie and you liked the comment, they will ask you why and accuse you of attracting other people's attention.

## They try to limit your freedom

This can happen on so many levels, but it's very common in possessive relationships. They will blame you for staying home instead of going out with friends. They invite themselves so there is no time without them. Or they might ask who they're messaging or unfollow someone on social media.

# CHAPTER FOUR

## They accuse you of betraying them

This is important! I have dealt with it in past relationships. If you don't tell them there's someone new at your workplace and they find out, they'll blame you for keeping it away from them. Even if you don't, you'll be the one apologizing because it makes them feel so bad for manipulating you and hurting them.

## Emotional instability

Possessive people in relationships cannot control their emotions. This is another reason they feel the need to control you. They fly off the handle with the smallest ones. You might have a nice night, but if you do something small like answering the phone, they'll get mad or freeze you, so beg your pardon

## They only count on you

Possessive people tend to have a small, if not empty, circle of friends. They are so focused on you and your relationship because they have nowhere else to go. They put all their needs, desires, and attention on you and expect the same from you.

## CHAPTER FIVE

## Conclusion

When you see this possessive behavior in your relationship, it's time to stop making excuses and do something about it. A possessive relationship is never a healthy relationship. No matter how long ago, relationships without trust and boundaries are not good for anyone. It can easily get out of control and dangerous. While it is understandable that a possessive partner's behavior stems from insecurity and fear, it is not correct. This understanding will help you talk to your partner without making excuses for their actions. To stop this possessiveness, you need to tell them how you feel. You should let your partner know that you love them and want the relationship to work, but you need boundaries and trust in order for them to feel safe with you The best thing you can do when you're in a possessive relationship is to go to couples therapy, encourage your partner to go to therapy alone, and figure out what caused these behaviors in the first place. This desire to control is usually so deeply ingrained in the past that it is difficult to break and change this pattern of possessiveness without help. If your partner is unwilling to make the effort or make those changes, it is time for you to do something. They may apologize and promise to get better, but their actions are usually repeated without proper guidance. That's when it's time to stand up. You deserve a healthy, respectful relationship based on trust, but not this ownership relationship. We must realize that love does not always conquer all. Being in a possessive relationship will only negatively affect your life and future.

www.ingramcontent.com/pod-product-compliance
Lightning Source LLC
LaVergne TN
LVHW020537160826
845677LV00015B/4112

* 9 7 9 8 8 4 8 9 4 6 1 1 6 *